Compact English
For Short-term Students

Book 1

Judy Lugton

Nelson

Thomas Nelson and Sons Ltd
Lincoln Way   Windmill Road   Sunbury-on-Thames
Middlesex TW16 7HP

P.O. Box 73146   Nairobi   Kenya
P.O. Box 943   95 Church Street   Kingston   Jamaica

Thomas Nelson (Australia) Ltd
19–39 Jeffcott Street   West Melbourne   Victoria 3003

Thomas Nelson and Sons (Canada) Ltd
81 Curlew Drive   Don Mills   Ontario

Thomas Nelson (Nigeria) Ltd
8 Ilupeju Bypass   PMB 1303   Ikeja   Lagos

© Judy Lugton 1978

First published 1978
ISBN 0 17 555216 9

Printed in Hong Kong

Contents

Teachers' Notes

Compact English Books 1 and 2 have been written as a number of structurally progressive situations in which students may find themselves. The aim is to improve spoken English.

The main purpose of the book is to encourage the students to practise outside the classroom the language they learn in it. Therefore whenever possible take them out to use the language they know. For example in any units using directions, send the students out in pairs to ask someone where a certain place is. Older students can be sent to the place and have to work their way back. In a shopping situation, take them to a shop and get each of them to buy something, e.g. a postcard. Extend the classroom activity by getting them to write on the postcard and send it to a friend or relative. This would necessitate their going to a post office. When teaching a travelling situation, take them on a journey by bus or train and get them to buy their own tickets. In a cooking situation, get them to ask an English person for his/her favourite meal and how to cook it.

When doing Unit 6, suggest that they make a survey of popular hobbies with their English families. After they have done Unit 8, take them out to ask people the way to a certain place. For Unit 20, they could make a survey of each other's future professions. When doing Unit 15, take them out to a shop or store and get them to describe the clothes.

Encourage them to learn as much as possible about the place where they are staying and about the British way of life. For younger and more elementary students this may be more difficult, so drawing, painting, cutting out pictures and other activities which they enjoy, can be arranged in the classroom so that they can also make use of the language they are learning. These could include practical occupations such as: cleaning their shoes, making a sandwich, making a 'whip' (simple dessert), which would involve their having to ask for certain articles and explain what they are doing.

For all levels and ages use comics, magazines and other things that appeal to them, as long as they are still using or learning English. The more students are put in practical situations that make them use their English, the more confident they'll be about using it on their own.

The plays should be used for acting out. Don't expect the students to remain in their chairs and read out their lines. Most young people enjoy acting. It helps to improve their intonation as they usually lose their inhibitions when acting out roles. With children, the use of costumes (or just hats) helps to make it more enjoyable.

The naming of characters with letters has been used in the dialogues and plays to make them more flexible. However, do get the students to give themselves names and develop the character of the person they are playing, e.g. in Book 1, Unit 18:

> A: Hello. How are you?
> B: Hello Pedro. I'm fine. How are you?
> A: Oh I'm fine too. This is Manuela.

Get the students to practise the lines after you have said them, and then divide them into groups after further practice. The teacher should be moving from group to group helping and correcting while they are practising.

Use games in the class for further practice and to provide some fun and competitiveness. Songs are also an excellent way of consolidating work.

Acknowledgements

The songs 'The Beggar' and 'The Animals' Helper' are taken from **Dialogues and Songs**, Book I, by Peter Bostock, published by Thomas Nelson & Sons Ltd.

Suggested Lesson Plan – using Unit 3 as an example

A INTRODUCTION

1 Pictures	Pictures of objects belonging to professions.	Elicit from students the vocabulary of professions, and using pictures elicit which object belongs to which profession.
2 Objects	Collect an object from each student.	Teach 'Whose is this?' and 'It's my ....' using your own object.
3 Verbal situation	A family going on holiday.	Mr S. took his maps, Mrs S. her camera, son his penknife, daughter her sunglasses.

PRACTICE

1 Chorus drill	Get students to repeat together the sentences you say.	It's his gun. It's her pen. It's his helmet.
2 Student/student practice	Students to ask and answer questions.	A: Whose pen is this? B: It's my pen. A: Whose pen is this? B: It's his pen.
3 Substitution drill	Get each student in turn to change the sentence by substituting another word.	It's ⎰ his ⎱ maps. It's ⎰ her ⎱ camera. It's ⎰ their ⎱ suitcases.

READING AND WRITING

READING AND WRITING	Write up on board what has been practised.	Get students to read it before writing it.

B CONSOLIDATION

B CONSOLIDATION	Look at first exercise in book or family tree.	Get students to repeat the sentences or ask and answer each other about the different relationships.
	Draw up own family tree.	

FREE STAGE

FREE STAGE	Get students to tell you about their own family.	Each student to give short talk on own family.

C HOMEWORK

C HOMEWORK	Use family tree in book.	Make up six sentences.
	Draw their own family tree.	

UNIT 1

Verb 'to be' and adjectives

Hello, I'm Pierre

Hello, I'm Mary

A: Hello, Pierre.
B: Hello, Mary.

A: How are you?
B: Fine thanks and you?
A: Fine thanks.

How are you?

I'm fine.   I'm tired.   I'm hot.

Where do you come from?

I'm Spanish.   I'm French.   I'm Swiss.

I'm Italian.   I'm Yugoslavian.

| A: Are you English? | A: Are you Italian? |
| B: No, I'm Spanish. | B: Yes, I am. |

1 ....French?
   No, ...German.

2 ....English?
   Yes, ...

3 ....Spanish?
   No, ...Italian.

4 ....Yugoslavian?
   Yes, ...

UNIT 2

Verb 'to be', present simple

This is John.
He's English.
He lives in England.
He speaks English.

This is Chantal.
She's French.
She lives in France.
She speaks French.

I'm ....
I'm ....
I live in ....
I speak ....

Who are you?
A: I'm Maria. I live in Madrid.
B: Where's Madrid?
A: It's in Spain.

I'm ....
I live in .... (town) in .... (country)
I speak...................... and ....

Song: One Man and his Wife

One man and his wife live in York in England.
One man and his wife live in York in England.
Two men live in York, live in York in England.
Two men, one man and his wife live in York in
   England.
Three men live in York, live in York in England.
Three men, two men, one man and his wife live
   in York in England.
Four men ....
Five men ....
Six men ....
Seven men...
Eight men ....
Nine men ....
Ten men...

This form must be completed before arrival.		
	First Name	Family Name
Name		
Nationality		
Address		
Age		
Passport No.		
Signature		

UNIT 3

Possessive adjectives

Mr Sparrow

Mrs Sparrow

John Sparrow

Mary Sparrow

Mr Sparrow:
Mrs Sparrow is his wife.
John Sparrow is his son.
Mary Sparrow is his daughter.

Mrs Sparrow:
Mr Sparrow is her husband.
John Sparrow is her son.
Mary Sparrow is her daughter

John Sparrow:
Mrs Sparrow is his mother.
Mr Sparrow is his father.
Mary Sparrow is his sister.

Mary Sparrow:
Mrs Sparrow is her mother.
Mr Sparrow is her father.
John Sparrow is her brother.

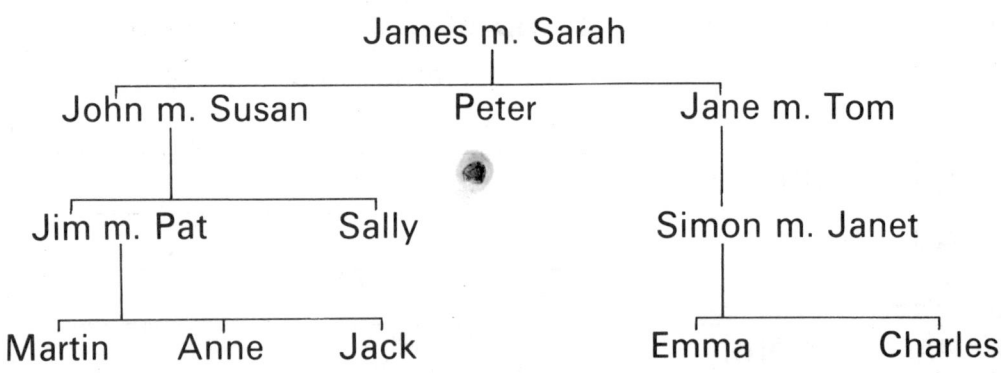

This is the Taylor's family tree. It shows you who married who (m. = married), and you can work out who are cousins, aunts, fathers, grandmothers, etc.

John, Peter and Jane were the children of James and Sarah.

Ask each other questions, e.g. 'Who is Sally's uncle?' 'Who is Janet's cousin?'

Draw your own family tree.

UNIT 4
'Have got'

A : Have you got any sisters?
B : Yes, I've got two sisters.

A : Have you got any brothers?
B : Yes, I've got one brother.

A : Have you got any sisters?
B : No.

a dog   **a cat**   **a bird**

a fish   **a horse**

A : Have you got any pets?
B : Yes, I've got ....

UNIT 5

'What . . . . like', verb 'to be' and adjectives

What's he like?

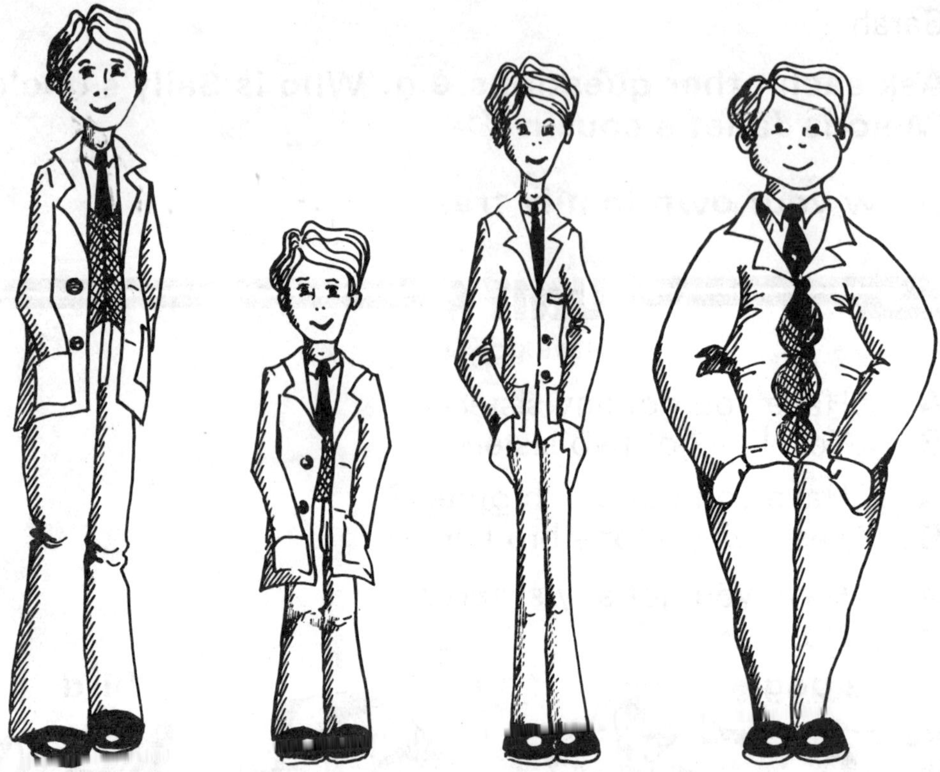

He's tall. He's short. He's thin. He's fat.

He's dark. He's fair.

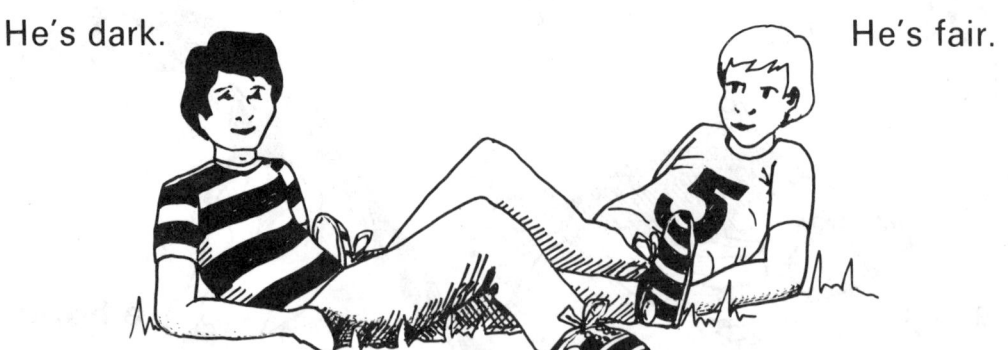

A: What's he like?
B: He's got blue eyes and fair hair.

Verb 'to like' and gerund

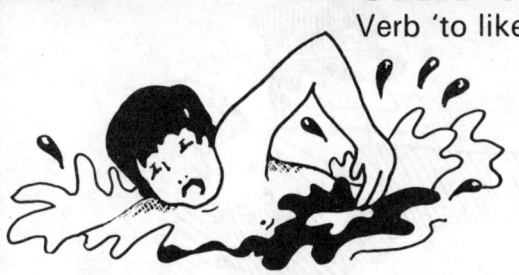

Pedro likes swimming.   Maria likes sewing.

John likes cycling.   Chantal likes painting.

Do you like   **walking?**

Do you like

reading?

Do you like   **playing the guitar?**

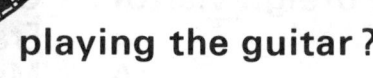

Do you like   **listening to music?**

A: Do you like walking?
B: No, I don't like walking,   A: Do you like reading?
    I like sleeping.   B: Yes, I do.

Play: The Parcel

*(Enter postman carrying a parcel. Knocks on door.
A opens it)*

A :	Yes?
Postman :	Excuse me, I've got a parcel. It's got an address. This address. But it's got no name on it.
A :	Oh, just a moment. (*calls*) It's the postman! (*Enter family and foreign visitor*)
B :	What's the matter?
A :	He's got a parcel with an address on it, but no name.
Foreign visitor :	Is it for me? Is it from my mother?
C :	It's big.
D :	Is it a book?
E :	Oh no! I don't like reading.
Foreign visitor :	Where does it come from?
Postman :	It comes from Italy.
Foreign visitor :	Oh. (*disappointed*) I come from France.
A :	My sister lives in Italy.
B :	I speak Italian.
E :	Oh Goodness! (*to postman*) Open it. (*Postman opens parcel. All look*)
D :	Oh it's a snake! (*All scream*)
Foreign visitor :	I'm glad it's not for me.
E :	It's not for any of us. (*closes door on postman*)
Postman :	What can *I* do with it?

A : Where's Birds Avenue please?

B : Take $\begin{Bmatrix} \text{the first} \\ \text{the second} \end{Bmatrix}$ turning $\begin{Bmatrix} \text{on the left.} \\ \text{on the right.} \end{Bmatrix}$

A : Where's $\begin{Bmatrix} \text{the post office} \\ \text{the cinema} \\ \text{the police station} \end{Bmatrix}$ please?

B : It's in Birds Avenue.

15

A : Where's the swimming pool please?

B : It's in London Street.

C : It's opposite the cinema.

D : It's next to the station.

E : It's by the river.

Draw a map of your own town.

16

Numbers and time

One	1	six	6	eleven	11	sixteen	16	thirty	30
two	2	seven	7	twelve	12	seventeen	17	forty	40
three	3	eight	8	thirteen	13	eighteen	18	fifty	50
four	4	nine	9	fourteen	14	nineteen	19		
five	5	ten	10	fifteen	15	twenty	20		

The train arrives at 2.15.

The train leaves at 2.55.

The bus leaves at 3.45.   The bus arrives at 4.08.

A: What time does the train leave please?
B: It leaves at 2.55.

When we talk about the time we say:
nine o'clock
a quarter past eleven
five past one
twenty past nine
a quarter to twelve
**but on timetables for buses, trains and planes
you find the time written like this:**

09.00
11.15
13.05
21.20
23.45

London	10.05
Oxford	11.11
Hereford	13.51
Manchester	15.48
Birmingham	16.09
London	17.28

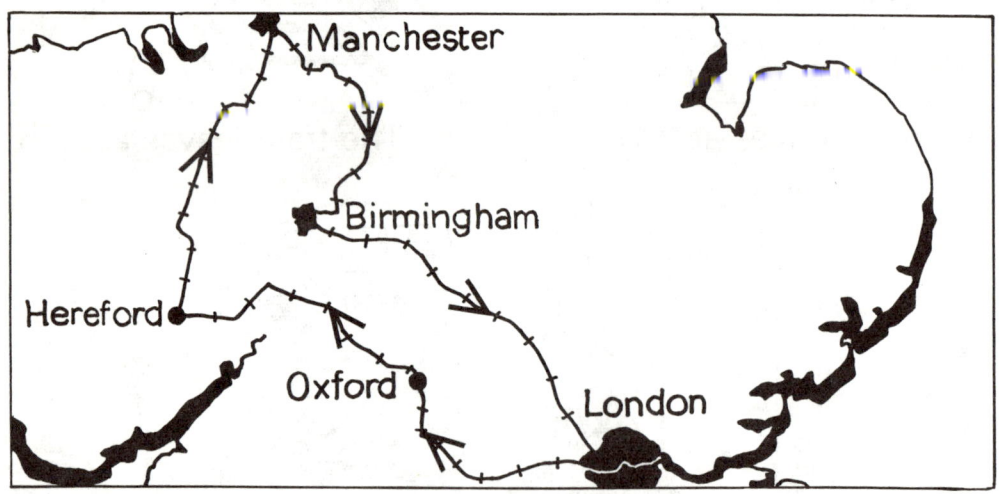

What time does the train leave London?
It leaves at ....
What time does the train leave Oxford?
It leaves at ....
What time does the train arrive in Hereford?
It arrives at ....

UNIT 10
Verb 'to do'

A:	Does this bus go to Merry Street?
Conductor:	No, it doesn't.
A:	Does it go to Oxford Road?
Conductor:	No, sorry.
A:	Well does it go to Birds Avenue?
Conductor:	Yes, it does.
A:	Oh good. (*gets on*) How much is it please?
Conductor:	Five pence. But why are you going to Birds Avenue and not Merry Street or Oxford Road?
A:	I want to visit one of my friends. One lives in Merry Street, one lives in Oxford Road and one lives in Birds Avenue.

Play: Directions

Foreign visitor:	Excuse me, where's the post office?
A:	It's near the church.
B:	No, it's in Dover Street.
C:	No, it's by the river.

Foreign visitor:	Oh dear!
A:	Take the first turning on the right.
B:	No, take the second turning on the left.
C:	No, take the 29 bus to Birds Avenue and …
Foreign visitor:	The 29 bus?
	(*Enter D*)
D:	Can I help?
Foreign visitor:	I want to go to the post office.
D:	Oh well, take the 13 bus to the museum.
Foreign visitor:	The museum?
B:	No, take the second turning on the left.
A:	Take the first turning on the right.
C:	But it's by the river.
A:	What do you want at the post office?
Foreign visitor:	Some twelve-pence stamps.
B:	Oh, I've got four. Here they are.
Foreign visitor:	Oh thank you very much. Here's forty-eight pence. Now it doesn't matter where the post office is.

UNIT 11

Present continuous

What's he doing?

He's eating.

What's she doing?

She's telephoning.

What are they doing?

They're reading.

What's he doing?

He's sleeping.

What's she doing?

HELLO!

She's talking.

What are they doing?

They're writing.

Pedro's eating a cake.

Sergio's writing a letter.

Rosa's drinking a cup of coffee.

Juan's reading a book.

Pierre's eating a sandwich.

Present continuous

A : **What's everybody doing?**
B : Pedro's sleeping.
C : He isn't sleeping, he's fishing.

B : Chantal's reading.
C : She isn't reading, she's writing.

B : Maria and Luisa are cycling.
C : They aren't cycling, they're swimming.

A : What are you doing?
B : I'm thinking.

A : Oh. What are you doing now?
B : I'm writing.

A : What are you writing?
B : I'm doing my homework. What are you doing?
A : I'm … well … I'm not doing anything.

Act out a mime and ask the other students to guess what you're doing.

Play: An Incident

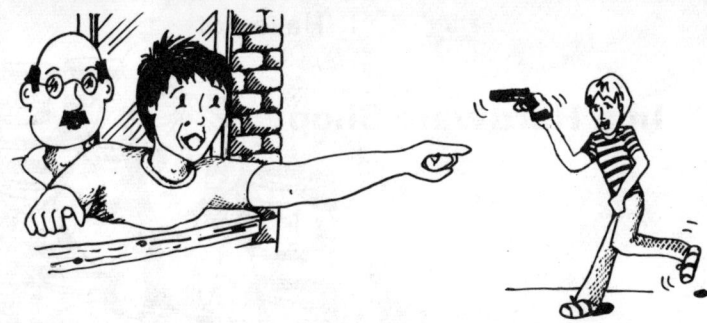

(*From a window*)

A : Come quickly! Look at that man in the street.

B : Which man?

C : Oh yes, I can see him. He's short and thin and he's got fair hair.

A : And he's running up the street.

B : Oh yes, he's carrying a gun.

D : What's happening?

B : There's a man running up the street.

C : He's coming up here.

A : Where is he? I can't see him.

B : I don't know.
   (*Enter man with gun*)

A :
B :
C : Oh!
D :

Man : Oh I'm tired. (*sits down*)

A : Who are you?

B : What are you doing here?

C : Are you a crook?

D : Why are you carrying a gun?

Man : It's OK. I'm a ...

B : Telephone the police!

Man : No. I'm ...
   Enter E

E : Ah there you are. Are you tired?

Man : Yes, acting is tiring.

A : Acting?

E : Yes this is Mark Green, the film star. We're making a film.

'Have got'

In a Hardware Shop

Shop assistant:	Can I help you?
Customer:	Yes, I want to paint my house. Have you got any white paint?
Shop assistant:	No, we haven't got any, but we've got some blue paint.
Customer:	Blue! Oh … well all right. Have you got any black?
Shop assistant:	No, I'm sorry, but we've got some red.
Customer:	Oh dear. Have you got any paint brushes?
Shop assistant:	No, we haven't.
Customer:	Well I can't paint my house then. And who wants a blue and red house?

In an English grocer's/baker's/greengrocer's/butcher's shop there are some ....s, but there aren't any ....s.

Adjectives and 'too' and 'enough'

It's **small**.   It's **big**.   It's **old**.

It's **new**.   It's **cheap**.   It's **expensive**.

A :   Do you like that dress?
B :   I don't know. Try it on.

It's too big.
It isn't small enough.

It's too short.
It isn't long enough.

It's too small.
It isn't big enough.

25

Vocabulary of food, 'I'd like'

Soup	Fish	Chops
Eggs	MENU	Omelette
Potatoes	Chips	Ice-cream

BILL		
	Soup	13p
	Chops	42p
	Ice-cream	15p
		70p
	Service:	7p
		77p

Waiter:	Can I help you?
Customer:	Yes please, I'd like the soup.
Waiter:	Yes?
Customer:	And the fish and chips.
Waiter:	Yes?
Customer:	And the ice-cream.
Waiter:	Anything else?
Customer:	Yes, coffee please.

A Recipe:

Vegetable Stew

2 large potatoes (chopped)
1½ cups carrots (chopped)
2 onions (chopped)
salt and pepper
seasoning

. . . .

1. Grate ¼ c. carrots and ½ onion into large casserole.
2. Brown 5 min. in butter.
3. Add 2 cups of water.
4. Bring to boil. (contd.→)

36

5. Add the chopped vegetables.
6. Add seasoning.
7. Cook until the vegetables are soft. Serve.

37

A: Let's make a stew.
B: O.K. We need some potatoes,

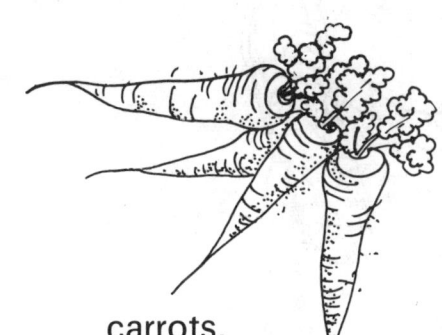

carrots,

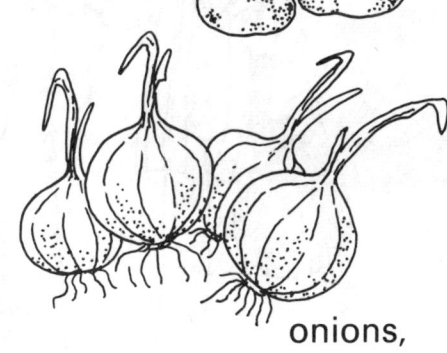

onions,

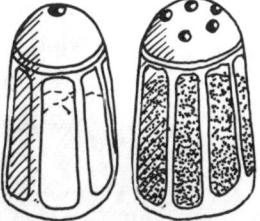

salt and pepper.

'Hope', 'think', 'sure' and future simple

A : Hello. How are you?
B : Hello A. I'm fine. How are you?

A : Oh, I'm fine too. This is C.
C : Hello B.

B : Are you English?
C : No. I'm …

A : He/she is staying with us for four weeks.
B : Oh good. I hope you'll enjoy yourself.

C : I'm sure I will.
A : Well, we're going shopping. See you later.

B : Yes come and have tea sometime. 'Bye.
C : 'Bye.

A : Do you think you'll go on holiday this year?
B :   I hope
         I think } I will.
         I'm sure

When I'm twenty-one I think I'll …………………………
When I'm twenty-one I hope I'll …………………………
When I'm twenty-one I'm sure I'll …………………………

28

Verb 'to want' and infinitive

What do you want to do today?

Do you want to go shopping?
Do you want to go to the shops?

Do you want to go cycling?

Do you want to go to the library?

Do you want to go swimming?

Do you want to go to the park?

A: Do you want to go swimming?
B: Yes I'd love to.

A: Do you want to go swimming?
B: I'd rather go to the cinema.

Mario loves reading.

Pedro hates reading.

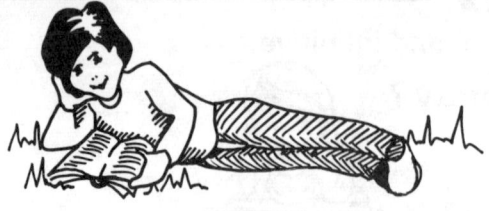

Maria loves reading but she prefers walking.

Tim loves Jill.

Jill likes Tim but she prefers David.

Stanislav loves cycling.

Pierre hates cycling.

What are your hobbies?
What do you hate doing?

UNIT 20
'Going to'

A : Where do you come from?

B : I come from
{ Huelva in Spain.
Rimini in Italy.
Bougival in France.
Zagreb in Yugoslavia. }

A : Why are you visiting England?
B : Because I want to learn English.

A : Are you going to learn English next year?
B : No, next year I'm going to visit France/Spain/
Italy/Yugoslavia.

When I'm Older

When I'm older I'm going to be ...

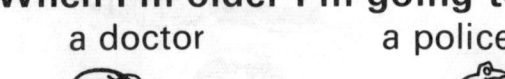

a doctor   a policeman   a model

a teacher   a librarian   a filmstar

Mike

Jane

Pat

Peter

John

Sue

When Mike's older, he's going to be a ....
Jane ....
Peter ....
Pat ....
John ....
Sue ....

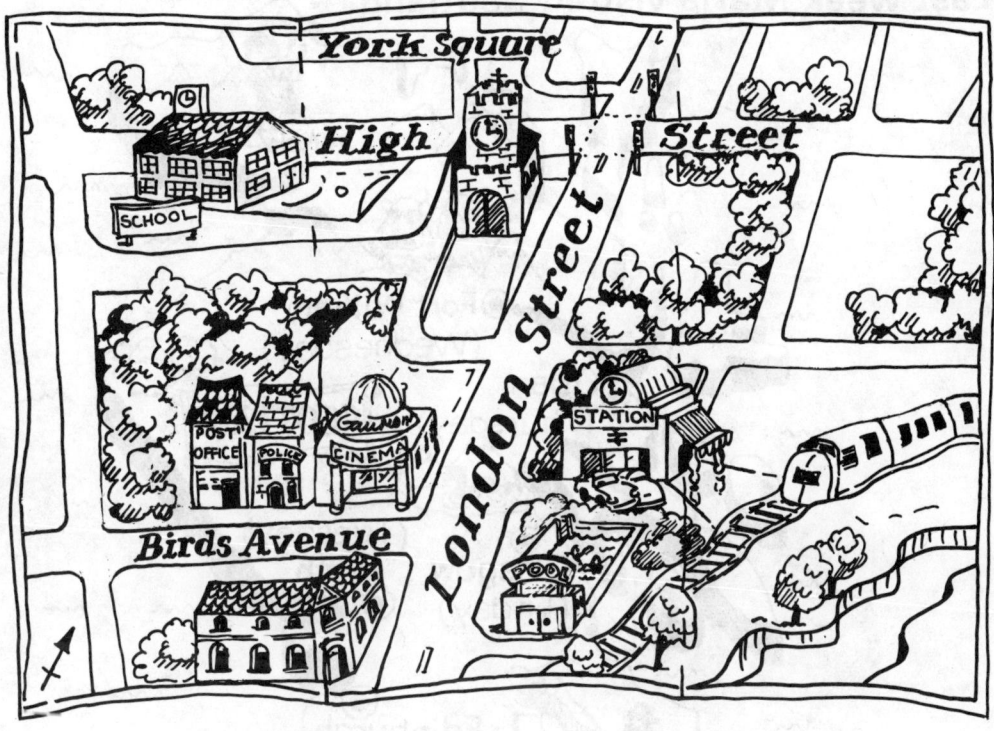

A : Excuse me, can you tell me the way to ,...... ?

B : Yes, take
$\begin{cases} \text{the first} \\ \text{the second} \\ \text{the third} \\ \text{the fourth} \\ \text{the fifth} \end{cases}$
turning
$\begin{cases} \text{on the right} \\ \text{on the left} \end{cases}$

and then take the...................................

Turn
$\begin{cases} \text{right} \\ \text{left} \end{cases}$
$\begin{cases} \text{at the traffic lights.} \\ \text{at the corner.} \\ \text{at the church.} \\ \text{at the cross-roads.} \end{cases}$

Walk
$\begin{cases} \text{up} \\ \text{down} \\ \text{along} \end{cases}$
Birds Avenue.

Draw a map of how you get to school from where you are living and then describe the route.

Past of verb 'to be'

Last week Maria visited Scotland.

On Monday she was in Edinburgh.
On Tuesday she was in Perth.
On Wednesday she was in Fort William.
On Thursday she was in Oban.
On Friday she was in Glasgow.

Manuel was ill last week and he didn't visit Scotland so:
On Monday he wasn't in Edinburgh.
On Tuesday he wasn't in Perth.
On Wednesday he wasn't in Fort William.
On Thursday he wasn't in Oban.
On Friday he wasn't in Glasgow.
He was in London, in bed.

Last year the Sparrow family visited America.

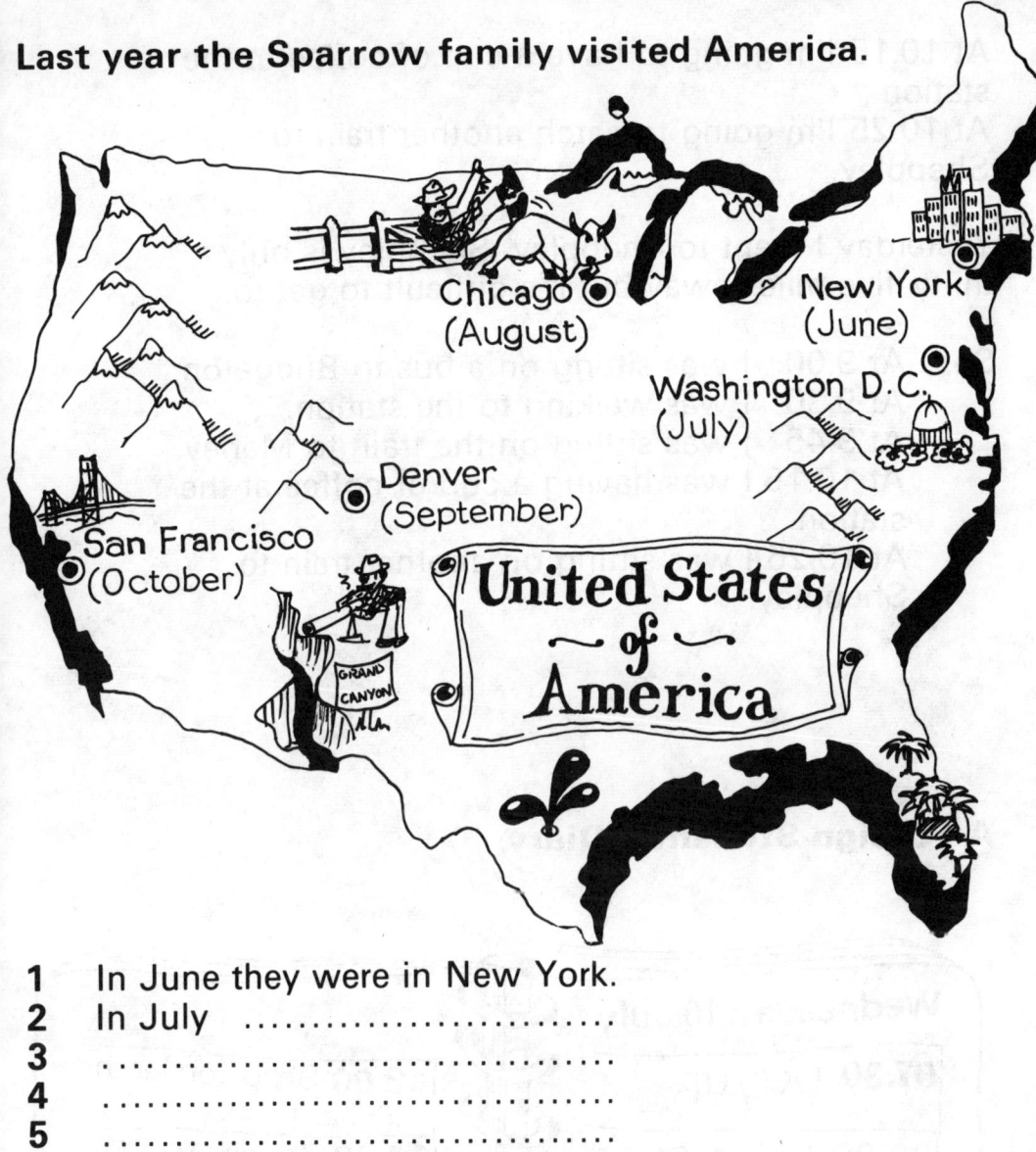

1 In June they were in New York.
2 In July ....
3 ....
4 ....
5 ....

UNIT 23
Past continuous

Tomorrow I'm going to Sheppley. Sheppley is only thirty-five miles away but it's difficult to get to.

So: At 9.00   I'm going to catch a bus to Bridgeton.
      At 9.30   I'm going to walk to the station from the bus stop.
      At 9.45   I'm going to catch a train to Marley Station.

At 10.15 I'm going to have a cup of coffee at the station.
At 10.25 I'm going to catch another train to Sheppley.

Yesterday I went to Sheppley. Sheppley is only thirty-five miles away but it's difficult to get to.

So: At 9.00   I was sitting on a bus to Bridgeton.
At 9.30   I was walking to the station.
At 9.45   I was sitting on the train to Marley.
At 10.15 I was having a cup of coffee at the station.
At 10.25 I was sitting on another train to Sheppley.

A Foreign Student's Diary

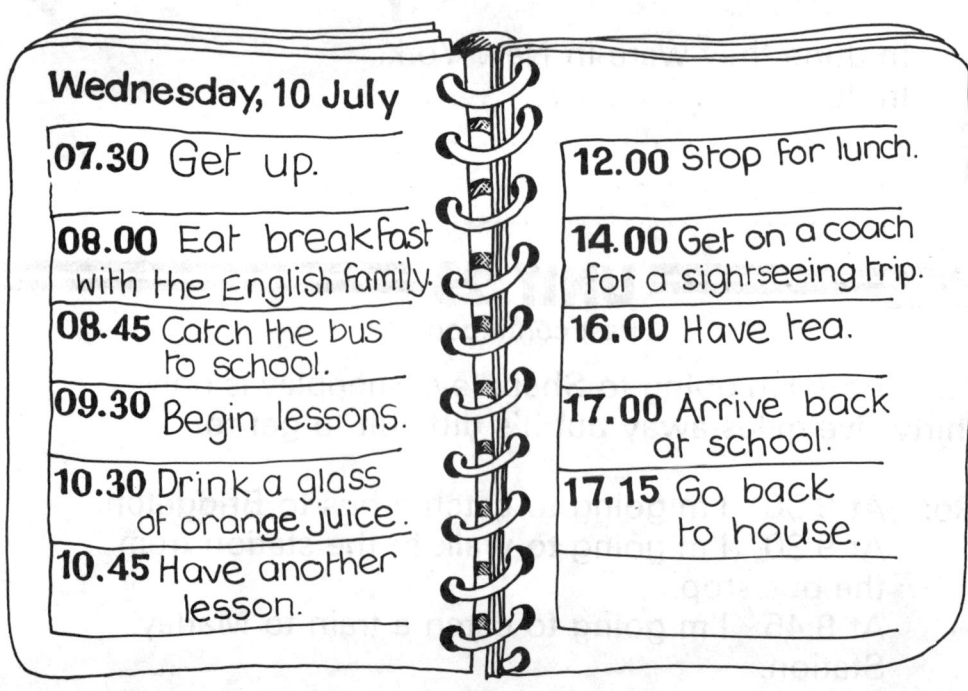

Wednesday, 10 July

07.30 Get up.

08.00 Eat breakfast with the English family.

08.45 Catch the bus to school.

09.30 Begin lessons.

10.30 Drink a glass of orange juice.

10.45 Have another lesson.

12.00 Stop for lunch.

14.00 Get on a coach for a sightseeing trip.

16.00 Have tea.

17.00 Arrive back at school.

17.15 Go back to house.

Song: The Beggar

I was walking,
I was talking,
I was laughing with a friend of mine,
When I saw him,
He was crying,
Then he looked up and caught my eye.

He was begging on the corner,
Living like a gypsy man.
He was shouting out a warning,
When the policemen came.

They were walking,
They were talking,
They were joking with the passers-by,
When they saw him,
He was crying,
Then he looked up and caught their eye.

He was begging, etc.

He was moaning,
He was groaning,
He was cursing at the cloudy sky,
When they took him,
He was crying,
Then he looked round and caught my eye.

He was begging, etc.

Play: The Bus Station

Foreign visitor:	Excuse me, can you tell me which bus goes to Sheppley?
Bus conductor:	Yes, that one over there. (*points*)
Foreign visitor:	What time does it leave?
Bus conductor:	At a quarter past four.
Foreign visitor:	Thank you. (*gets on bus*)
	(*Enter C*)
C:	Excuse me, what time does the bus to Sheppley leave?
Bus conductor:	At a quarter past four. It's over there.
C:	Oh thank you. (*gets on bus*)
	(*Enter D*)
D:	Excuse me, I want to go to Sheppley.
Bus conductor:	You want to catch that bus over there.
D:	Thanks. (*gets on bus*)
	(*Bus conductor gets on bus*)
Bus conductor:	Tickets please.
Foreign visitor:	A single to Sheppley please.
Bus conductor:	Twenty-five pence please.
C:	Return to Sheppley please.
Bus conductor:	Fifty pence please.
D:	Why aren't we moving?
Bus conductor:	There's no driver.
C:	Where's the driver? It's twenty past four.
Bus conductor:	I don't know. Oh here he is.
	(*Enter driver*)
C:	We'll be late getting to Sheppley.
Driver:	I'm sorry, this bus isn't going to Sheppley. It's broken down.
Foreign visitor:	Can I have my money back?
C:	And me?
Driver:	Of course.
D:	What are we going to do?
Driver:	Go by train.
	(*All sigh and get off the bus*)

'There is', 'there are', 'some and any'

A: What are you making?
B: I'm making a stew.

A: There are lots of potatoes in it. There aren't many carrots in it.

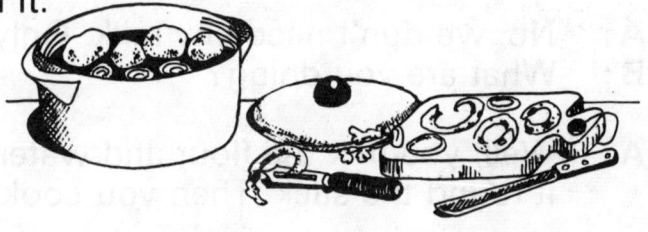

A: What are you making?
B: I'm making soup.

A: Ugh! It needs more salt and there isn't enough pepper.

A : This is a very easy recipe. Is the fire lit?
B : Yes. What do we do? I'm hungry.

A : We need some jam and a stick.
B : Here's some jam and is this stick all right?

A : Yes that's fine.
B : Here's some butter.

A : We don't need any butter. We need some flour though.
B : Here's the flour. Oh, I'm hungry! Do you want some milk?

A : No, we don't need any milk. Only water.
B : What are you doing?

A : Well, you mix the flour and water and then wrap it round the stick. Then you cook it over the fire.

B : What happens then?
A : You pull out the stick and fill the hole with jam.

B : Oh.
A : Well here's the stick. You do the cooking. I'm going home for lunch.

UNIT 26

'Any/many', 'lots/much' and adverbs

A : Are there many bananas?
B : Yes, there are lots of bananas.
Yes, there are lots.

A : Are there many oranges?
B : No, there aren't many oranges.
No, there aren't many.

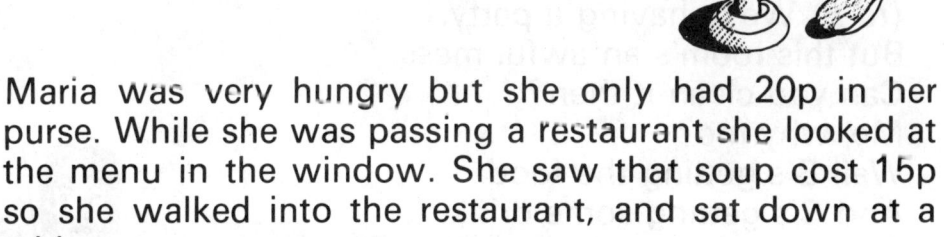

A : Is there any sugar in the bowl?
B : Yes, there's plenty.

A : Is there any sugar in the bowl?
B : No, there isn't much.

Maria was very hungry but she only had 20p in her purse. While she was passing a restaurant she looked at the menu in the window. She saw that soup cost 15p so she walked into the restaurant, and sat down at a table.

A waiter asked her what she wanted and she ordered the soup. He nodded and walked away slowly. She waited and waited, and thought hungrily about the soup. At last the waiter appeared with the soup, but when he got to her table he turned round and whispered quietly to another waiter, and he poured some of the soup onto Maria's dress.

She screamed loudly and walked to the restaurant door angrily, but the manager saw her and said, 'I'm very, very sorry about your dress. Please have a free meal.'

So Maria had a grapefruit, roast chicken with peas and potatoes, and lots and lots of ice-cream. When she left the restaurant she felt very, very full.

Play: The Party

A: Let's have a party.
B: Oh yes!
C: What shall we do?
A: (*to B*) Well, we need food. Can you get some food?
B: Yes, O.K.
C: We need drink.
A: Yes. Can you get some Coca Colas?
C: All right.

(*Enter D*)
D: What's happening?
B: We're having a party.
D: Oh good! I can bring my guitar.

(*Enter E*)
D: (*to E*) We're having a party.
E: But this room's an awful mess.
A: Can you clean it then?
E: Me; why me?
A: Well B's getting the food.
B: And C's getting some drink.
D: And I'm bringing the music.
E: (*to A*) And what are you doing?
A: Well, I'm doing the thinking.

Past simple of regular verbs

When he was young he wanted to be a success.
  He studied hard at school,
  he worked hard in an office,
  he travelled a lot,
and now he's an important business man.

When he was young he didn't care about anything.
  He didn't study hard at school,
  he didn't learn anything,
  he didn't work hard,
  he didn't travel,
and now he's a poor man.

Yesterday John went to London to see the Queen.

9.00   He got up.

9.30   He had breakfast.

10.15   He went to the station.

10.20   He bought a ticket.

10.30   He caught a train.

11.45   He got to London.

12.00   He saw the Queen.

What did you do yesterday?

What time did you get up on Sunday?
What time did you have breakfast on Sunday?
What time did you have lunch on Sunday?
What time did you go to bed on Sunday?

Past simple of irregular verbs

Last Monday

He built houses.

Last Sunday

He didn't build houses.

She taught.

She didn't teach.

He sold newspapers.

He didn't
sell newspapers.

He made cars.

He didn't make cars.

She wrote
for a newspaper.

She didn't write
for a newspaper.

**Collect pictures of people at work and explain
what they did yesterday.**

Song: The Animals' Helper

My friend Klaus
Kept a house
For lonely animals.
He had some dogs,
He had some cows
And they didn't give him
Any trouble.

He was the animals' helper,
And he gave them some food
And some shelter.

They didn't pay rent,
They came and went
And told exciting stories.
There were some birds,
There were some cats
But they didn't give him
Any worries.

He was, etc.

Then one day,
The fourth of May,
The weather was bright and sunny.
He met some bears,
Some big, black bears
And they didn't have
Any money.

He was, etc.

The bears stayed there
For many a year
And didn't forget the moral.
They gave some love,
They took some love
And they didn't have
Any quarrels.

He was, etc.

Customs Officer:	Good morning. How long are you staying in England?
Foreign visitor:	About a month.
Customs Officer:	I see, um. What will you do here?
Foreign visitor:	I want to learn English. I'm going to study here.
Customs Officer:	I see. Which school are you going to?
Foreign visitor:	Oh, the Sheppley School of English.
Customs Officer:	Right, and where are you going to stay?
Foreign visitor:	I'm going to stay in Sheppley with a family.
Customs Officer:	And when are you leaving the country?
Foreign visitor:	On August 31st.
Customs Officer:	Good, that's all. Enjoy your stay.
Foreign visitor:	Thank you.

Make up questions to ask other students from this passage.

Charles Martinson was born in 1915. When he was young he wanted to be famous. He wanted to be a politician or a filmstar. His uncle died when he was fifteen and left him a little money. In 1935 he went to the United States of America. He found a job as a gardener for a film director. He wanted the director to make him into a film star. He worked very hard in the garden, but he didn't become a film star. Then he got a job as a gardener for a politician, but he didn't become a politician. After fifteen years he was a very good gardener and a lot of people wanted him to work for them. Now he's an old man, and he's very famous. Not because he's a film star or a politician, but because he knows more about gardening than anyone else.